SANDY PEOPLES

Sandy Peoples
EmotionsSheWrotePoetry

Acknowledgement

I want to thank everyone who took the time to help me make this possible. I couldn't have done it without all the wonderful people who lent a helping hand. Germancreative for the book cover, Ben McGrath for the blurb, AllAboutYouCoachingLLC, and all my family and friends. With my sincere gratitude, I thank you.

Table of Content:

If Miracles Happened
I'm Coming Home
It Has To End
Is It Me
I've Been There
Judgment Day
Lord
Love
Loving You
Memories
Missing You
Mother
My Feelings
My Life
My Love
My Sons
Regrets
Relationships
Scared 7 Year Old
Still In Love With You
That Night
The Call
The Pain In My Heart
Thoughts Of You
Wedding Day
What I Have
What They Don t Know
What's Wrong With Me
Where We Go
Where You Belong
Who Am I

Table of Content:

America Cries

Awaken and turn
    On television
    Structures going down is
    All in our vision

Loved ones
    lamenting and crying
    Watching individuals, so many
    Hurt or dying

Kids headed to sleep without
    Fathers or mothers
    Presently to fear conflict is
    Going to take their brothers

America Cries

People with signs that read
  "Someone is missing"
  No one has time to pause
  And Pay attention

Frighteningly going to sleep
  Every night
  Soon our soldiers will be sent
  Into battle to fight

This country was once
  Free
  Left with sorrow, longing for
  Peace

BRINGING UP THE PAST

I thought I knew you
   From inside out
   After tonight, I am faced
   With Doubt

You acted so irately
   You made me feel low
   I no longer trust you
   This I know

Why did you behave this way
   I'm not sure why
   I'm over the suffering
   I will no longer cry

BRINGING UP THE PAST

You bring him up now and
　　That is wrong
　　Why at this time
　　It's been so long

There is no way for
　　Our love to last
　　As long as you keep
　　Dwelling on the past

CONFUSED

Although I have someone who
   Cares
   I can't stop thinking of the
   Nights we shared

I initially said I love you
   But I need to be clear
   Now I love only two

He treats me great
   He goes above and beyond too
   He does things for me
   You never would do

CONFUSED

Sometimes I wonder if anything
   Is it meant to be
   Is it him and I or
   You and me?

I can't let him go
   Why oh why do
   I still love you so

DEAR JESUS

Anytime I need a friend
   I know where to go
   You won't turn your back
   When I am at my low

You assist me
   Every single day
   Because of my faults
   You had to pay

Sometimes I'm quite busy
   I don't pause to pray
   I'm aware my errors
   Won't run you away

DEAR JESUS

I thank you for taking
   My sins away
   I am grateful to you
   Every single day

DON'T GO

I want you to know
  I can't let go
  I won't move
  I need you to know

I still can't explain why
  We have reached the end
  I lost it all
  I lost my best friend

I will never forget
  The times we shared
  What brought us here
  Why don't you care?

DON'T GO

I make a wish for each
   Star I see
   I'm hoping you'll come back
   To me eventually

I wish you were here
   One last night
   I can't believe it's over
   After one brief fight

What went wrong
   I'm still unsure
   I will beg if I have to
   Don't exit the door

DON'T JUDGE ME

Why do you criticize me
   Observing the outside
   Try gazing to see instead
   The secret the body hides

Spend time getting to know me
   From the inside out
   You'll understand who I am
   What I am all about

I might be a little heavier
   But perhaps you do
   Have your own imperfections
   Inside you too

DON'T JUDGE ME

What if I walk in a
   Different way
   We are all unique and
   That is okay

My thoughts may be scattered
   I may not have a career
   At least I'm not one of those
   Buying drugs or beer

Let's be concerned with
   Our own lives
   Words have a lasting impact
   They slit like knives

EMOTIONS

I'm overcome with emotions
   When I see you with her
   I remember how we were
   Forever you swore

I look back one last time
   To see if it is true
   I have my answer as I see her
   Stand by you

As I step outside
   In my eyes form a tear
   I never thought losing you
   Would be something to fear

EMOTIONS

I begin moving slowly
   Along the street
   Knowing I will never have you
   This is a defeat

I will try to block you
   From the heart
   It's time to move on and create
   A fresh start

FAMILY

Mom was there
   To help me through
   When I had a problem
   She knew what to do

My father was gone
   Since I was born
   Yet after he died
   I still mourned

Grandma was present till
   The end
   She was in fact my
   First friend

FAMILY

My sister and I used to
   fight
   But as we've gotten older we
   Remain tight

My brother has always
   Been there
   He helps me when life
   Seems unfair

My family, I love with all
   My heart
   There to the end, and there
   From the start

FEELINGS HIDDEN

I lay in bed and think
   Of you the entire night
   If it was my decision, you
   Would be holding me tight

My feelings for you
   Must not show
   I can't tell. No one
   Can know

I wish I could
   Shout it out
   My love for you
   I attempt to doubt

FEELINGS HIDDEN

When I see you
   Myself I betray
   Fantasizing of being
   Together one day

Being with you, I am aware
   It is only a dream
   No matter how genuine
   It may seem

FORBIDDEN LOVE

Angels above us are aware
　　Of my prayers
　　To love you more with every
　　Layer

Stars in a deserted
　　Sky
　　Hear all my forbidden
　　Cries

I may be selfish they
　　All would say
　　But what would I give
　　To have a day

FORBIDDEN LOVE

Heartbroken but I know
   It is true
   That I can never truly
   Have you

Giving up, no longer
   Will I do
   Forbidden or not, I still
   Want you

GONE

Drinking and dancing
   You left that day
   I should have stopped you
   Made you stay

I at least advised you to
   Go slow
   I had that feeling you should
   Not go

After finishing my evening
   I headed to bed
   Disturbed by the call
   You were dead

GONE

I hit my knees
   You paid the price
   The night was fun
   But took your life

At the funeral people
   Looked at me to blame
   I help my head down
   Nothing but shame

I should have stopped you
   Not let you leave
   I no longer have you
   Please let me greave

Drinking is fun
   Driving it not
   Taking your keys
   Would have changed a lot

GONE AWAY

We don't know why
   People go astray
   Is it so wrong for us to
   Want them to stay

I am aware they are in a
   Better place
   Although, it is very difficult
   To face

I know I will see them
   In a different life
   Where they are free from
   Pain, sorrow, or strife

GONE AWAY

We have to say goodbye
    Today
    In my heart, you will forever
    Stay

GRADUATION

Sons, daughters, sisters
  And brothers
  Took the stage
  One after another

Nervous and excited
  It is the end
  Leaving teachers, halls,
  Coaches, and friends

They address everyone
  By name
  So variety, yet still
  The same

GRADUATION

Standing tall, proud of
    One another
    Time to move on
    To go a little further

Time to throw our caps
    In the air
    Photographs, hugs, and
    Farewell

HAVE YOU FOUND THE ONE

While lying in his arms
   At night
   Do you wish someone else was
   Holding you tight

When he looks at you and says
   I love you
   Do you say it back or just an
   I do too

When he says he loves you
   From the bottom of his heart
   Are you still thinking of the
   One who had it from the start

HAVE YOU FOUND THE ONE

When he says," We will
    Be together till the end."
    Do you think likely
    As just friends

If you do all this
    Above
    It isn't
    True love

Have you found
    The one like you say
    If not, release and simply
    Walk away

HEARTBROKEN

The days are becoming longer
   Nights are too
   And all I can think about is
   How much I want you

As I sit here all alone
   I understand and now see
   You did not love me
   Never did you want me

I now feel saddened
   The one who is unable to sleep
   How did I let my feelings for you
   Get so deep?

HEARTBROKEN

Considering and watching
   The vehicles pass by
   How did this occur
   How come you lied

I'm unsure why I want
   To see you
   Aware that you never loved me
   What did I do

You enjoy yourself
   Each day
   And I sit here inconsolable
   I wish you had stayed

HELP

I came upon an elderly woman
   While walking down the road
   So very brittle, alone, and
   cold

She halted saying "I'm shortly
   going to die"
   I could tell her voice
   did not lie

She was shivering cold
   Tears in her eyes
   With one look at her, I
   Began to cry

HELP

She looked at me and
  Said so clear
  Death is something I do
  Not fear

I asked her if her family
  I could call
  She said she had no family
  At all

She needed help
  I could tell
  I needed to move quickly
  No time to fail

I brought her to the ER
  To see what was wrong
  I told her to hold on
  And be strong

Her life continues
  Now on her way
  I check up on her
  Every day

HE'S MINE

You took him from me
   Wrong thing to do
   You will pay
   Why does he love you

I will take him from you
   You watch and see
   He is not yours
   He belongs to me

He feels terrible when you cry
   I have no pity
   The whole thing is a lie

HE'S MINE

You have no love for him
   That's plain to see
   When this is over, he
   Will be with me

You control him
   Cause a lot of fights
   That's okay
   It ends tonight

HURT

You passed by with her
   On your side
   I tried to fake it, but the
   Hurt, I could not hide

You were content
   I could tell by the expression
   How can you be over me
   Here starts the depression

You were aware of how much it hurt
   You saw tears in my eyes
   I hope you treat her better
   I hope you prevent the cries

HURT

She was cheerful, happy,
   And in love
   She seemed to believe you
   Were sent from above

I wanted you to leave
   I was miserable to the core
   You looked at me proudly as
   You walked toward the door

All we've been through
   The times we have shared
   Everyone had finally seen
   You couldn't have cared

IF MIRACLES HAPPENED

If miracles happened, I would
    Be the first in line
    My wish would be for you
    To be mine

If miracles happened, I would
    No longer cry at night
    I would be in your arms
    Holding on so tight

If miracles happened, there would
    Be no lies
    I would stop having to hear the
    Word goodbye

IF MIRACLES HAPPENED

If miracles happened, you would still,
   Be with me
   You wouldn't doubt your
   Love for me

They, in fact, do
   Come true
   It was a miracle that I
   Got to love you

IM COMING HOME

I assumed I had issues
   I had to get away
   I had time to reflect and
   I'd like to return home today

I simply felt I
   Had it bad
   Because I never paused to
   Consider what I had

I discovered I couldn't run
   I have to confront my fears
   I have to face them
   Battle with tears

You are the person that
  Helped me through
  I couldn't have done it
  Without you

I love you with all
  Of my heart
  I hope this is the last time
  We are apart

I am sorry I went so far
  Away
  But, Mom, I'll be home
  Today

IT HAS TO END

I adore you
   As a friend
   But these nighttime pleasures
   Must come to an end

You see, I love him
   With every piece of my heart
   I don't know why I
   Let this start

He is the only one
   Who has the key
   So it can no longer
   Be you and me

IT HAS TO END

Don't misunderstand me
   I enjoyed our nights
   I now must do
   What is right

If we continue it will
   Hurt both of you
   Which is something I never
   Intended to do

I'll never forget the
   Times we had
   I hope I can fix it
   Before something gets bad

IS IT ME

Seeing you with her
   Breaks my heart
   But, I knew about your marriage
   From the start

When I am in your arms
   I know it won't last
   I will soon be part
   Of your past

When you are with her
   Are you thinking of me
   When you shut your eyes
   Is it me you see

IS IT ME

When you look at me
   In my eyes
   Are you holding on to
   Our last goodbye

Do you desire my presence in
   Your life everyday
   If not, goodbye is all I
   Shall say

I'VE BEEN THERE

At first, it starts
   Out great
   Candies, flowers, and
   Ideal dates

Starts having excuses of
   Where he has been
   Supposed to arrive at seven
   He shows up at ten

You know in your heart
   That he cares
   Your heart is overflowing with him
   It starts to tear

New memories you have
   Are of crying
   Your use to the tears, no-shows and
   Of lying

He is never present
   Always gone
   He is constantly whispering on
   The phone

Probably a female
   To replace you
   Just know I've been
   Through this too

Eventually, he will be
   Taken away
   You will be begging
   Him to stay

I know this because as he walked
   Out my door
   You thought he was perfect
   As he walked into yours

It is okay
   You didn't know
   I'm trying to help you
   Time to let go

JUDGMENT DAY

You committed a crime
   Sentenced to jail
   Guilty or not
   They set the bail

You did the crime
   Going to prison
   Jury and a judge
   Will make the decision

You will have to face it
   Everyone will hate
   The only thing to anticipate
   Is a release date

Put you away
   From the rest

JUDGMENT DAY

Keep you safe we
Will try our best

You did the crime
It is time to pay
Put behind the bars
You chose this way

LORD

When I asked you
   In my heart
   You replied " Now we
   Shall never part"

I know that no matter where I go
   Or what I do
   I will always
   Have you

You keep an eye on me
   From above
   Providing me with all I need
   Especially love

LOVE

Love is something amazing
  Not found every day
  Sooner or later, you discover
  It along the way

It holds a meaning
  For you and I
  The love for you
  Never die

No one could ever
  Take it away
  When it's there, it's there
  To stay

Sometimes you try to fight it
   And keep it in your heart
   But once you love someone
   You never want to be apart

We have to be grateful to our
   God above
   For providing us with something as
   Wonderful as love

LOVING YOU

Why did I have to fall in love
    With you
    After seeing what you
    Put other females through

Why trust you
    With my heart
    Why take it
    And tear it into parts

When I see you, I know it won't
    Be long
    You're just making me love you
    And dragging me along

Someday I hope
   That you could see
   No one could ever
   Love you like me

MEMORIES

Today I can't seem to get you
   To exit my head
   On days like this, it's difficult to
   Get out of bed

I recall your sweet touch
   And our lives together
   I miss you so much

On those lonely nights
   You would draw me to you
   And hold me so tight

You had this unique way
   It is all coming back to me
   Why today

I gave you my heart
  Given back, all torn
  In separate parts

I told myself I could get
  Over you
  I couldn't forget you
  Deep down, I knew

You were my life,
  All that I had
  Alone with these memories
  Missing you shall I add

MISSING YOU

Day after day, I think of you
   Both good and bad times
   We have been through

Since you left and now gone
   I question what happened and
   How it went wrong

If you could see
   The tears I have cried
   But the tears come from you
   All of your lies

I wonder what you're doing tonight
   Who the lucky girl is that you're
   Holding tight

Often I want to
   Stop playing these games
   It is over now, I must
   Face it today

You are happy
   I can see
   You love her
   It is no longer me

MOTHER

Your love is pure, honest,
  And true
  In a world full of hate I want to
  Thank you

There to always brighten
  My day
  Having the right thing
  To say

You taught me all
  I needed to know
  You watered me with love
  To help me grow

I know too soon your life
   Came to an end
   I love you, Mother,
   My best friend

MY FEELINGS

My feelings intensified
  When I saw you today
  I tried to fight them,
  To bury them some way

In a relationship, I
  Can see
  Why couldn't you have
  Chosen me

Your dark hair
  Your brown eyes
  One look at you, my heart
  Start to die

When you're around, I am
   Unable to speak
   When you are near
   I get so weak

I can't move on
   I won't ever
   I will love you
   Forget you never

MY LIFE

I can still smell the past
   In the air
   The walks, dances, bonfires,
   And fairs

Now replaced with
   Anger and strife
   I'm becoming old
   That's just life

I remember wishing
   Years away
   Replaced with wanting back
   The old days

When I didn't have consequences
   For my actions
   Or when rumors began, causing
   No significant reaction

What is there to do
   Alone and down
   Nothing to do
   In this small town

I feel like life has
   Passed me by
   I am lonely and sad
   No matter what I try

MY SONS

To my sons, I love
   So dear
   Daddy strayed away for
   Some beer

Mommy is here to take care
   Of my boys
   To love, care, and buy
   Them toys

When they grow up, they will see
   Why mommy cried
   All the times that
   Daddy lied

I hope they grow up to
   Loving him after the hell
   The way it looks no
   One can tell.

REGRETS

If I could have seen
   What I had
   I didn't realize
   I just stayed mad

You were here by my side
   Day and night
   All I ever wanted to do was
   Argue and fight

If you were here
   Beginning a fresh start
   I would tell you I love you with
   Every piece of my heart

Can you please forgive me
   One day you might
   I'm sorry I hurt you
   I want to make this alright

RELATIONSHIPS

All types of relationships
  Some good, some bad
  Some make you happy
  Some make you sad

Some you get to spend time with
  And see every day
  Some are only phone calls because
  They are far away

Some are great and filled with
  Excite
  Some bring agony, but others
  Only fight

Some have a very great
   Start
   Some will eventually break
   Your heart

You can not know how they will
   Go
   Will they end
   Only time knows

SCARED 7 YEAR OLD

It makes me shiver
   It makes me shake
   It is worse than
   An earthquake

I can't understand what is
   Going on
   I'm afraid we'll
   Die before long

Daddy has now left
   For the sea
   Why did he leave
   Mommy and me

At school, some big
   People say
   It killed thousands
   That day

I hope they don't take me
   I am only seven
   If something happens I
   Will see you in heaven

STILL IN LOVE WITH YOU

My feelings for you
   I am not always willing to show
   When I am near you
   My emotions continue to grow

It broke my heart when
   We were apart
   Yet I still love you with
   All of my heart

Now you returned but
   I have someone new
   He is wonderful but
   No one can replace you

You run through my mind
   Day and night
   I still miss your arms
   Holding me tight

I know I still have memories
   But that's not enough
   I desperately want you
   Why is it so rough

I will get over you
   Just not today
   In my heart is where
   You'll stay

THAT NIGHT

Thoughts of you still
   Gather in my head
   I remember that night
   I recall what you said

You played with my mind
   You begin to flirt
   No care at all who
   You would hurt

I remember leaving your bed
   At daylight
   The memories of all we did
   That night

As a tear falls from
   My eyes
   I know your words were nothing
   But lies

I can forget you and move
   On with my life
   You severely wounded my heart
   Brought me only strife

THE CALL

At first, I thought it was
   Going great
   Until you called me that
   Night late

You said all we ever
   Do is fight
   The love we had,
   Ended tonight

I never imagined what
   You had to say
   I was hoping this would
   Go a different way

Was there anyone else there
   Someone new
   You told me this was
   Coming from you

This is unbelievable
   You crushed my heart
   Lying on the floor in
   Tiny part

THE PAIN IN MY HEART

I know you said it was over
   Even though I don't understand why
   I accept that you said
   Your final goodbye

You said it's for the best
   No longer my knight
   Seeing you on a daily basis
   To now out of sight

Oh, how I miss you
   You all that I had
   I couldn't imagine it
   Would end so bad

I imagined my heart
   You would not break
   I never thought this pain
   I could mentally take

I pray, I cry, I plead to
   God above
   That one day, he could
   Send back my love

THOUGHTS OF YOU

Outside, things are getting bad
   I wonder what your doing
   I wonder if your sad

I wish you were here
   So I could stop
   Shedding tears

I have no idea how
   We fell apart
   But I know I love you
   With all of my heart

Every time I hear our song
   I sit and wonder what
   Went wrong

When I see you, I
   Know I will cry
   I can't fight the tears
   But at least I will try

WEDDING DAY

Today is the day
   We say," I Do."
   Today is the day to
   Make it true

We will look into each
   Others eyes
   As everyone else stands
   And sighs

For now, we are a couple and
   A team
   No matter how surreal it
   May seem

Now we will dance the
   Night away
   Baby, it is us as one
   After today

WHAT I HAVE

Some people are starving
   Some sick and dying
   While I sit here crying
   Over some little lie

People are being beaten
   Day and night
   While I sit here regretting some
   Small fight

Some people have one
   More day
   While I sit here wishing you
   Would have stayed

I need to thank God
  For all I got
  I could lose it all
  Which is a lot

WHAT THEY DON'T KNOW

According to my friends
  I'm too good for you
  They have no idea
  What we've been through

You are made fun of
  They claim your bad
  They don't know you
  It makes me so mad

No one understands how much
  You care
  Or all the memories that
  We have shared

I don't care how they feel
  Or what they say
  They will fall in love and
  See one day

WHATS WRONG WITH ME

One minute I am happy
   One minute I am blue
   I don't know how to
   Live without you

I am either sobbing or
   Depressed
   What is wrong with me
   Is this a test

The entire world starts
   To criticize me
   Look at your life and
   Allow me to be

I feel like screaming
  What is the use
  Why care
  Nothing to lose

What is wrong with me
  I have no idea
  The doctors can't fix it
  They just hand me a pill

WHERE WE GO

The 12 years appeared
   To go by slowly
   The last year,
   Time to grow

It is time to go on
   With life
   To start a career, be a mother
   A wife

Leaning in to say
   Goodbye
   I will see y'all shortly
   I promise to try

Going away to face
   The world
   I can do anything says
   The Lord

For I am no longer a
   Little child
   Things will be hard
   No longer mild

I can do it on
   My own
   Sure help I will need
   Farewell and so long

WHERE YOU BELONG

In your arms is
  Where I long to be
  Waking up near you is
  What I long to see

Daydreams and fantasies
  Seem to be untrue
  But prayers and faith might
  Bring me closer to you

A gentle smile, hello and
  A kiss
  Would be my
  Ultimate bliss

Open your heart and take
   A chance with me
   You might see I am
   What you need

WHO AM I

I am a girl chasing
   Hopes and dreams
   No matter how unreal
   They may seem

I am a girl seeking
   Love and affection
   I won't take the risk
   Scared of rejection

I am a girl who sometimes
   Strays on days
   Consequences I do have
   To pay

I am a girl who has
   A genuine heart
   Although, I let others
   Rip it into parts

I am a girl my mother
   Raised well
   Through my actions this
   You can tell

WHY

Why do I still have
   This pain in my heart
   So long it has been since
   We fell apart

Why do I still set
   And cry
   Can't we give it
   Another try

Why do I still think
   Of you day and night
   I wish we could have
   Made this right

Why do I still love
  Why do I feel so low
  I can't make myself
  Let you go

WHY NOT ME

I want you back
  With me again
  Those stunning eyes
  That gorgeous grin

Every time I see you
  My heart departs
  Why can't we rewrite the story
  Have a fresh start

Everything you embrace
  Is a gift from above
  In my heart, you stay
  Forever my love

You told me you love her
    I know I can see
    I wish it were different
    If only it were me

YOU AND I

You and I are only one
   Step away
   The feelings I have, I
   Want them to stay

You and I will join
   As a couple
   Long walks, candle
   Light suppers

You and I both won't be aware
   When will it be
   Before long, it will be
   You and me

For the time being, we
   remain friends
   In the near future, it will
   Be you and I in the end

For now, I will wait for
   You to see
   Together we are
   Meant to be

YOU GAVE IT ALL

When I thought it
  Was the end
  You gave me a
  Friend

When someone broke
  My heart
  You offered me a love
  To start

When I was lacking things
  And got mad
  You helped me to realize
  All I had

When someone I
  Loved died
  You assured me it was
  Okay to cry

YOUR GONE

Sitting here contemplating everything
   We've been through
   I'm realizing how much
   I want to be with you

It feels like you are miles away
   I hope to see you soon
   I can't wait for that day

I can't believe you're
   Actually gone
   My heart is so empty, I feel
   Completely alone

I thought I knew you
   Thought you would not lie
   If you could see the
   Tears that I've cried

I did not think we would be apart
   You may not be in my arms
   But will always be in my heart

A POEM FROM ME TO YOU

Sincerely, I appreciate you
   Reading about my life
   Many can identify with
   All the love and strife

Always make sure
   To get emotions out
   Venting any way you can
   Is what it is all about

Pick up a pen and paper
   Begin to write
   Your personal universe
   No one in sight

I convey my love to everyone,
   Everywhere
   I hope you enjoyed this book
   Take Care.

ABOUT THE AUTHOR

Sandy Peoples is a poet, writer, professional life coach, and much more. She began composing poems at a young age and started expressing her emotions. She is regarded as one of the top ten Emotional Intelligence Coaches. She enjoys reading, writing, and spending time with loved ones.

She is the owner of AllAboutYouCoachingLLC. Her company strives to assist others to transform their life, become the person they have always desired to be, and realize their full potential.

She has had a difficult life and is now living her best life. "If possible for me, it is for you as well."

Contact Sandy to transform your life from good to outstanding.

Allaboutyoucoaching.org
   allaboutyoucoachingl@yahoo.com

About

EMOTIONS SHE WROTE POETRY

This collection of poems discusses love, friendship, life, faith, and tragedy. You will be able to relate to this simple poetry. Knowing that someone else has experienced something gives you comfort. As a life coach, I wanted to put what I preached into practice. Since I was a small child, I have wanted to publish a poetry book, and I have now made the decision to do so. I appreciate you for assisting me in achieving my objective.